COLOGNE GUIDE 2023

Explore, Enjoy, and Discover |

Top Attractions and Local Tips

Rita R. Nowlin

Table Of Content

CHAPTER 1: COLOGNE OVERVIEW

Welcome To Cologne

Cologne, in the heart of Germany, is an intriguing city where history, culture, and modernity blend harmoniously. Stacey, an experienced traveller with a voracious curiosity, was drawn to this dynamic metropolis, anxious to discover the wonders hidden inside its cobblestone streets and iconic sites.

A rush of adrenaline coursed through Stacey's veins as her jet touched down at Cologne Bonn Airport. When she arrived in Cologne, she was welcomed by a symphony of architectural marvels, a monument to the city's rich history. The beautiful Cologne Cathedral ascended into the sky like a silent guardian of time, with its complex Gothic spires. Stacey was enthralled by its majesty, staring in wonder as she absorbed the weight of its centuries-old history.

Stacey walked into the Altstadt, the historic old town, along small streets adorned with colourful half-timbered houses that seemed to tell their own stories. She was drawn to local cafés and eateries by the aroma of freshly baked pretzels and the hum of lively discussion, where she indulged in traditional German specialties and enjoyed laughter with friendly locals.

Stacey's journey took her to the calm Rhine River banks. She discovered the Hohenzollern Bridge, which is ornamented with love locks and offers stunning views of the town. Stacey realised, as the sun set below the horizon, sending a warm glow over the river, that

Cologne's charm wasn't just in its physical beauty; it was in the way it made her feel—welcomed and accepted.

Stacey was also deeply influenced by the city's lively cultural environment. She saw a mesmerising concert of classical music at the Cologne Philharmonic, where the notes appeared to fill the very air around her. The stunning collection of contemporary art at the Ludwig Museum stirred her mind and inspired debates about creativity and expression.

Stacey's trip to Cologne turned out to be more than simply a vacation; it was a journey of self-discovery and connection. She found herself forging a link with a city that easily balanced its past and present in the middle of historical grandeur and modern marvels. Stacey knew that as her time in Cologne came to a close, she would take the memories of this incredible voyage with her, forever grateful for the experiences that had filled her soul in ways she had never imagined.

Brief History

Cologne's history, which spans two millennia and is located on the Rhine River in western Germany, is rich and diversified. The city, originally as Colonia Claudia Ara Agrippinensium, was founded by the Romans in the first century AD and swiftly developed in significance as a significant commerce and administrative centre. The Roman influence may still be seen in the shape of the city and some of its historical relics, such as the Roman Dionysus mosaic.

Cologne became an important ecclesiastical centre during the Middle Ages, with the massive Cologne Cathedral, a marvel of Gothic architecture that took years to build. Because of its strategic location, the city became a crossroads for commercial routes, and its wealth and cultural impact flourished.

Cologne became an economic powerhouse in the nineteenth century, thanks to its proximity to the Rhine, which facilitated the rise of manufacturing and transportation businesses. However, due to its industrial importance, the city suffered greatly during World War II, resulting in significant devastation.

Many historical landmarks were restored after the war, and Cologne regained its role as a dynamic cultural and economic powerhouse. It is currently known for its thriving artistic scene, diversified population, and major festivities like as the Cologne Carnival.

Culture And Traditions

The cultural legacy of Cologne is strongly established in its historical significance. With a history that dates back over two millennia, the city is rich in customs that have withstood the test of time. The Cologne Cathedral, one of the city's most recognisable monuments, is not only a work of Gothic architecture but also a symbol of the city's devotion to its religious heritage. The annual Kölner Lichter festival, which features a spectacular fireworks show over the Rhine River, is a modern incarnation of Cologne's long-standing tradition of commemorating its history.

Traditions are also integrated into the fabric of daily life in Cologne. The local Kölsch beer, a pale and crisp brew, is more than just a beverage; it represents the city's social and convivial attitude. Traditional pubs, known as "Brauhäuser," in the city offer a genuine experience where locals and visitors alike may savour the local beer and indulge in substantial regional food.

Throughout the year, cultural events and festivals abound, showcasing the city's artistic richness. The Cologne Carnival, often known as the "fifth season," is a stunning extravaganza of parades, costumes, and music that represents the city's energetic and cheery personality.

CHAPTER 2: TRIP PLANNING

Best Time To Visit

The greatest time to visit this wonderful city is between late spring and early autumn, precisely between May and September.

Cologne enjoys nice weather throughout this season, with temperatures ranging from 15°C to 25°C (59°F to 77°F), making it suitable for experiencing the city's numerous outdoor attractions. The beautiful Cologne Cathedral, the quaint Old Town, and the scenic Rhine River are best enjoyed when the weather is pleasant and suitable to walking tours and outdoor activities.

Furthermore, this time period corresponds with a number of cultural events and festivals that highlight Cologne's colourful energy. During the Kölner Lichter (Cologne Lights) event in July, guests are treated to a stunning fireworks show over the Rhine River, which is accompanied by music and entertainment. Open-air concerts, flea markets, and outdoor dining options are also available during the summer months, allowing tourists to immerse themselves in the local culture.

It's also worth mentioning that the summer months are peak tourist season, which means more people and higher hotel expenses. For those looking for a more tranquil experience, the shoulder months of May and September provide a fair balance of pleasant weather and less tourists.

In contrast, the winter months can be frigid, making many outdoor attractions less enticing. However, the city's festive Christmas markets, which take place from late November to December, are a beautiful experience that draws people in with their attractive ambiance, seasonal delights, and one-of-a-kind crafts.

Travel Essentials

- Begin by dressing appropriately for the weather, as the city has a temperate temperature. Pack layers and diverse clothing because the weather might be unexpected. Don't forget to bring suitable walking shoes because Cologne's charm is best experienced on foot.

- The UNESCO World Heritage-listed Cologne Cathedral is a must-see destination. Remember to bring your camera to capture the breathtaking architecture and delicate details. Cologne is also known for its eau de cologne, so save some room for a scented souvenir.

- A well-equipped travel guide or map can be extremely useful for navigating the city's historic streets. A power bank is a useful item for keeping your devices charged so you can take photos, access maps, and stay connected.

- While most tap water is safe to drink, owning a reusable water bottle is both environmentally friendly and practical. Exploring the local cuisine is a feature of any vacation, so make sure to pack any essential prescriptions and digestive assistance.

- If you intend to visit museums or other sites, find out if advance reservations are required owing to crowd control measures. A little rucksack will be useful for transporting your things while exploring.

- Finally, to enrich your cultural experience, become acquainted with local habits and terminology. Knowing a few basic German phrases can help you connect with locals and navigate day-to-day encounters.

Transportation To And In Cologne

Travelling by rail provides not only comfort and efficiency, but also breathtaking vistas of the German countryside. High-speed trains, such as ICE and Thalys, provide speedy connections to major cities like as Frankfurt, Amsterdam, and Paris, making it an attractive choice for travellers who want to visit various locations. Cologne also has an international airport, Cologne Bonn Airport (CGN), with well-connected flights for people travelling from afar. If you're already in Europe, though, taking use of the huge rail network can be a memorable and efficient way to get to this dynamic city noted for its gorgeous cathedral, rich history, and cultural attractions.

Using Cologne's enormous public transit system is one of the most famous methods to get around the city. Trams, buses, and trains connect the city's key attractions in an efficient and well-connected network. The KölnCard, a popular tourist option, gives guests unlimited access to several means of transit, allowing them to easily navigate the city's crowded streets.

A boat down the Rhine River is a necessity for a memorable and gorgeous experience. This method of travel not only provides beautiful views of Cologne's skyline, but also highlights the city's architectural wonders, such as the magnificent Cologne Cathedral. The calm flow of the river and the ability to see the city's monuments from a different angle make for a wonderful and enjoyable voyage.

Cycling lovers will find Cologne to be a bike-friendly destination, with well-maintained bike lanes and bike-sharing programmes.

Exploring the city on two wheels offers for a more leisurely pace, allowing you to soak up the local vibe and discover lovely hidden places.

einen guten ...

CHAPTER 3:

ACCOMMODATION IN

COLOGNE

Recommendation For Various Budget Levels

Exploring Cologne's attractiveness does not have to be expensive for budget-conscious visitors. Begin with a trip to the famed Cologne Cathedral, a Gothic masterpiece with free admission. Stroll along the picturesque Rhine River promenade for free, taking in the city's splendour. With its narrow alleyways and historic pubs serving affordable local cuisine and a vibrant environment, the Old Town (Altstadt) entices. Don't miss out on the Chocolate Museum, where a small admission price provides insight into the history of chocolate manufacture.

Consider getting a KölnCard, which provides access to public transport as well as discounts on numerous attractions. Explore the Ludwig Museum, which features modern art, and the Roman-Germanic Museum, which focuses on history. Enjoy tasty pastries at traditional bakeries and dinners at cosy neighbourhood restaurants without breaking the bank.

If you want luxury, Cologne will not disappoint. Pamper yourself with stays in opulent hotels with stunning views of the cathedral or the Rhine. Explore the high-end shopping along Hohe Strasse and dine at Michelin-starred restaurants. Enjoy a spa day at Claudius Therme, a luxurious thermal bath and health centre.

5 Luxury Hotel Suggestions

1. **Excelsior Hotel Ernst**. This opulent hotel features magnificent rooms and

suites, as well as an award-winning restaurant, a piano bar, and a spa. It is located in the centre of Cologne, close to the cathedral and the Old Town. The nightly rate begins at €250.

2. **Hyatt Regency Cologne**. This upmarket hotel features a sophisticated sushi restaurant, a trendy bar, a pool, and a wellness spa. It is situated on the Rhine River's banks, providing wonderful views of the city. The nightly rate begins at €200.

3. **Hilton Cologne**. This luxurious hotel features spacious rooms and suites, as well as a restaurant, a fitness centre with a sauna, and a business centre. It is in the city centre, close to the train station and shopping. The nightly rate begins at €150.

4. **Cologne Marriott Hotel**. This upscale hotel includes comfortable rooms, a

French-Asian fusion cuisine, a bar and a fitness centre. It is located across the Rhine River from the city centre in the Deutz district. The nightly rate begins at €120.

5. **Steigenberger Hotel Köln**. This luxurious hotel features spacious rooms and suites, as well as a gourmet restaurant, a bar and a spa. It is located in the centre of Cologne, close to the cathedral and the Old Town. The nightly rate begins at €100.

5 Mid-Range Hotels Suggestions

1. **Holiday Inn Express Cologne - Muelheim, an IHG Hotel**. This hotel lies in the Mülheim area, just a few minutes' walk from the Rhine River. It has modern rooms with free Wi-Fi, a

fitness centre, and a breakfast buffet. The nightly rate begins at €70.

2. **NH Koln Altstadt**. This hotel is located in the centre of Cologne, close to the cathedral and the Old Town. It has nice rooms with flat-screen televisions, as well as a restaurant and a bar. The nightly rate begins at €60.

3. **Motel One Koln-Waidmarkt**. This modern hotel is in the Neumarkt neighbourhood, just a few minutes' walk from the railway station. It has chic rooms with free Wi-Fi, as well as a 24-hour bar and a game area. The nightly rate begins at €50.

4. **CityClass Hotel Europa am Dom**. This hotel is in the centre of Cologne, just a few steps away from the cathedral. It has modern rooms with free Wi-Fi, a fitness centre, and a breakfast buffet. The nightly rate begins at €45.

5. **Ibis Koeln Am Dom.** This hotel is in the centre of Cologne, immediately across from the cathedral. It has comfortable rooms with free Wi-Fi, as well as a bar and restaurant. The nightly rate begins at €40.

Other Accommodation Options

1. **Hostels** are an excellent choice for budget travellers. They provide communal dorms as well as single rooms, and some even have kitchens. Prices begin around €20 per night.

2. **Apartments** can be an excellent choice for families or groups of friends. They provide more space and solitude than hotels and can be rented for extended periods of time. Prices about €50 per night.

3. **Bed and breakfasts (B&Bs)** are a more intimate alternative to hotels. Breakfast is usually included in the fee, and some even have private facilities. Prices begin around €60 per night.

4. **Guesthouses** are comparable to bed and breakfasts, but they provide a more hotel-like atmosphere. They usually have shared restrooms, however individual rooms are available. Prices begin around €70 per night.

5. **Camping** is an excellent choice for individuals who wish to be close to nature. Within a short drive of Cologne, there are various campsites. Prices begin around €20 per night.

Here are some more suggestions for seeking lodging in Cologne:

- Book your lodging ahead of time, especially if you are travelling during peak season.

- When selecting an accommodation choice, keep your budget and desired location in mind.
- Before making a decision, read evaluations of various lodging options.
- Be flexible with your trip dates and times, as this can help you get a better rate.
- Look for special offers and discounts, such as those provided by travel websites or the city of Cologne.

CHAPTER 4: COLOGNE'S TOP ATTRACTIONS

Cologne Cathedral (Kölner Dom)

Begin your journey by admiring the cathedral's magnificent façade. The statues' meticulous detailing and the grandeur of the entrance set the tone for the artistic beauty within. The immense interior area, with its towering nave, stained glass windows, and high-vaulted ceilings, will take your breath away as you come inside.

Climbing the South Tower of the cathedral is a must for panoramic views of Cologne. While the hike is difficult, the stunning views of the city and the Rhine River make it all worthwhile. The tower also contains the Cathedral Treasury, which includes a collection of valuable artefacts and sacred relics.

While exploring the interior, take time to see the spectacular stained glass windows, which represent biblical stories and creative designs that play with light in captivating ways. Another feature is the Shrine of the Three Kings, which is supposed to house the remains of the Magi who visited the newborn Jesus.

Attend a Mass or service in the cathedral for a spiritual experience. The long history of worship in this sacred room, combined with the organ's resonance, creates a poignant atmosphere.

Before you leave, stop by the Kölner Dom Museum to learn more about the cathedral's history and construction.

Ludwig Museum

When you go into the Ludwig Museum, you'll be lured to its incredible collection of pop art, abstract art, and expressionist masterpieces. The museum's rich collection of works by prominent artists such as Andy Warhol, Roy Lichtenstein, and Pablo Picasso offers a unique perspective on the evolution of art in the twentieth and twenty-first centuries.

One of the museum's attractions is its remarkable collection of Russian avant-garde art, which includes groundbreaking works by artists such as Wassily Kandinsky and Kazimir Malevich. Visitors can discover numerous styles and views thanks to the museum's attention to various artistic movements.

Don't miss out on seeing the spectacular architecture and design of the museum itself while you explore it. The clean, modern spaces add to the entire experience and provide a vibrant backdrop for the artwork.

Furthermore, the Ludwig Museum frequently offers temporary exhibitions that dive into specific themes, artists, or artistic movements, providing visitors with an opportunity to connect with new and thought-provoking content.

After you've had your fill of art, take a stroll along the gorgeous Rhine promenade just outside the museum. This place is ideal for rest and reflection, with breathtaking views of the Cologne Cathedral and city skyline.

Chocolate Museum

The rich aroma of cocoa envelops you as you enter, setting the mood for a journey through the history and artistry of chocolate creation. The museum's instructive exhibits walk you through the full chocolate-making process, from cacao bean farming to the meticulous workmanship involved in crafting delightful delights.

The interactive Chocolate Fountain, where you can dip marshmallows or fruit into a cascading cascade of velvety chocolate, is a highlight. The museum offers workshops where you may make your own personalised chocolates under the supervision of skilled chocolatiers for a genuinely hands-on experience.

The Chocolate Cinema at the museum carries you through time, illustrating the evolution of chocolate across many civilizations and epochs. Furthermore, the tropical greenhouse allows you to investigate cacao trees and learn about their function in chocolate manufacture.

Before you depart, don't forget to stop by the museum's café, which serves a variety of delectable chocolate treats and beverages. The gift shop is a treasure trove of mementos, featuring a wide range of excellent chocolates that you can take home with you.

Rhine River Promenade

This iconic waterfront resort, which stretches along the gorgeous Rhine River, offers a wealth of activities to make your vacation unique.

Begin your trip with a leisurely stroll along the promenade, where you'll be able to take in stunning views of the Rhine, the towering Cologne Cathedral, and the Hohenzollern Bridge. This region is especially beautiful at sunset, when the warm hues dance across the river and the spires of the church are illuminated.

Explore the Chocolate Museum, a sweet treat for all ages, to immerse yourself in a rich tapestry of culture. Discover the history of chocolate and watch the sophisticated chocolate-making process, all while sampling samples.

Visit the neighbouring Roman-Germanic Museum for a more in-depth look at history. This museum, which houses an array of artefacts dating back to ancient Roman times, provides insight into Cologne's origins as a Roman colony.

Take a picturesque river trip to enhance your experience. Drift down the Rhine, taking in panoramic views of Cologne's skyline, historic bridges, and charming neighbourhoods. These cruises provide a unique viewpoint on the city's splendour.

When hunger hits, the promenade's dining options range from cosy cafes to magnificent restaurants. Enjoy local cuisine while watching the boats float along the river.

Hohenzollern Bridge

- **Cathedral Views**: Take a leisurely stroll across the Hohenzollern Bridge for breathtaking views of the UNESCO

World Heritage Site Cologne Cathedral. Capture the stunning sight of the cathedral's magnificent Gothic architecture against the river's backdrop.

- The bridge is draped with innumerable "love locks," a ritual that has achieved international fame. Couples can participate in this romantic ritual by fastening their own lock to the railings of the bridge and throwing the key into the Rhine, symbolising their everlasting love.

- **River Cruise Observation**: Take in the bustle of life on the Rhine River as riverboats and cruise ships pass beneath the bridge. The juxtaposition of these yachts against the calm waters and the city skyline produces an enthralling spectacle.

- **Engage with local street performers and artists** who frequently congregate on the bridge, giving a colourful cultural experience. Enjoy live music, painting exhibitions, and performances that add to the colourful ambiance of the bridge.

- **Scenic Walks**: Take a peaceful walk along the Rhine Promenade to explore the nearby riverbanks. Enjoy the cool wind, scenic views, and a profusion of cafes and shops selling local specialties.

- **Capture Memories**: The Hohenzollern Bridge is an excellent location for photographers and Instagram users. The combination of old and modern components results in intriguing compositions.

Altstadt (Old Town)

Begin your trip with the renowned Cologne Cathedral, a UNESCO World Heritage site and Gothic architectural marvel. Admire its exquisite façade, climb its towers for magnificent city views, and experience its awe-inspiring interior.

Wander through the Altstadt's narrow cobblestone alleyways, discovering lovely squares and hidden jewels. Immerse yourself in the lively ambiance of Alter Markt and Heumarkt, busy hubs where locals and tourists alike go to enjoy traditional German food and beverages.

Discover history around every corner with a visit to the Roman-Germanic Museum, which displays artefacts from the city's pre-Roman settlement. Stroll across the Hohenzollern Bridge, which is ornamented with 'love locks' and provides a spectacular perspective of the cathedral and the Rhine River.

Indulge in some retail therapy in the city's premier shopping streets, Hohe Straße and Schildergasse, which feature a mix of international brands and local boutiques. Don't miss the small stores selling Cologne's characteristic fragrance, Eau de Cologne, for an authentic experience.

Relax on the Rhine's riverbanks, possibly enjoying a leisurely sail to admire the cityscape. And, as the evening sun sets over Altstadt, head to the busy pub and bar scene for a sample of the local brews and a chance to mix with the friendly locals.

Flora And Botanical Garden

Stroll through lush, manicured gardens displaying a diverse range of plant species from throughout the world. The Flora & floral Garden is a living tapestry of floral diversity, with themed parts such as the Mediterranean Garden and the Japanese Garden. Visitors can enjoy the splendour of exotic flowers, unusual trees, and tranquil water features, making it a sanctuary for photographers and nature enthusiasts alike.

The garden is also a focus for educational programmes. Botany, conservation, and sustainable gardening practises are explored in guided tours and workshops. It's a great way for families, students, and curious minds to learn about the intricate ecosystems that thrive inside the garden's confines.

The garden offers various covered areas for picnicking, reading, or simply soaking in the peace and quiet. The Flora building, a magnificent glass-and-steel structure, includes a restaurant where tourists can savour local cuisine while taking in panoramic views of the lush surrounds.

The Flora & Botanical Garden conducts events that highlight the changing seasons throughout the year.

CHAPTER 5:
NEIGHBOURHOOD
EXPLORATION

Innenstadt

Innenstadt, or "Inner City," is Cologne's core and captures the soul of this dynamic German metropolis.

The UNESCO World Heritage-listed Cologne Cathedral stands as a massive landmark of Gothic architecture and spiritual significance.

Its elaborate façade and soaring spires are breathtaking, and the interior contains beautiful stained glass windows and sacred relics.

As you walk along the cobblestone streets, you'll see ancient Roman walls and mediaeval gates set beside lively stores, cafes, and restaurants. The Belgian Quarter has a bohemian ambiance with independent retailers and creative flare, while Hohe Straße and Schildergasse offer superior shopping choices ranging from high-end boutiques to multinational names.

A short walk brings you to the Ludwig Museum, which has an extraordinary collection of modern art, including pieces by Picasso, Warhol, and Lichtenstein. The Roman-Germanic Museum, located nearby, dives into the city's Roman heritage, displaying artefacts such as the Dionysus mosaic.

Innenstadt also provides culinary delights for your taste senses. Traditional beer halls serve native Kölsch beer and substantial meals, but gourmet restaurants offer a blend of world flavours. The KölnTriangle's observation deck offers a panoramic view of the city skyline and the sweeping Rhine.

Ehrenfeld

The streets of Ehrenfeld are covered with colourful street art, which contributes to the neighborhood's hip and bohemian vibe. The Belgian Quarter, which is part of Ehrenfeld, is well-known for its fashionable boutiques, cosy cafes, and busy pubs. It's a sanctuary for shopping and foodies alike, with a broad selection of cuisines and handcrafted goods.

Ehrenfeld's commitment to the arts is one of its most notable characteristics. There are various galleries, studios, and cultural facilities in the neighbourhood that highlight the talents of local artists. The "Ehrenfelder Hopping" event, which occurs on a regular basis, allows visitors to explore these creative spaces and interact directly with artists, developing a closer connection to the local art community.

The dynamic spirit of the neighbourhood is likely most visible in its crowded outdoor markets, which provide fresh vegetables, artisanal wares, and vintage finds. The weekly flea market and the monthly Designers' Market are ideal places to immerse oneself in the welcoming atmosphere of the neighbourhood.

Südstadt

Südstadt, or "South City," is a vibrant district directly south of the city centre that invites visitors to immerse themselves in its intriguing environment.

Südstadt's architecture is a perfect combination of old and new, with wonderfully preserved ancient buildings coexisting with modern structures. Walking down its streets shows an eclectic mix of charming boutiques, cosy cafes, and friendly eateries catering to a variety of interests. The artistic energy of the district can be seen in the numerous galleries and street art projects that provide a creative flavour to the surroundings.

The Volksgarten, a lush green park offering a calm getaway from the urban bustle, is a landmark of Südstadt. Its tranquil roads, scenic ponds, and vibrant flowerbeds make it a great location for leisurely walks or picnics. Furthermore, Südstadt's proximity to the Rhine River encourages visitors to enjoy riverside promenades and stunning cityscape vistas.

Culture fans may also find something to enjoy. There are numerous theatres, music venues, and cultural centres in the neighbourhood that organise events ranging from live performances to art exhibitions. Exploring Südstadt also entails learning about its rich past, such as its function as a hub for numerous communities, each of which contributes to the district's distinctive character.

Belgian Quarter

The Belgian Quarter, also known as "Belgisches Viertel" in German, is known for its tree-lined alleys, old architecture, and a plethora of boutiques, cafes, and art galleries. As you walk along the cobblestone pathways, you'll notice a colourful tapestry of street art and graffiti adorning many buildings, adding to the neighborhood's bohemian vibe.

The bustling environment is one of the features of this quarter. The area is alive with activity as locals and visitors alike congregate at the numerous cafes, restaurants, and bars. The food scene here is wide and fulfilling, catering to all palates, with everything from traditional German fare to foreign cuisine.

Boutiques and vintage shops in the Belgian Quarter will also excite shoppers. This neighbourhood is a destination for fashion-forward people looking for one-of-a-kind clothing, accessories, and home decor products. The mix of upmarket boutiques and thrift stores creates the ideal mix of old and new.

The Belgian Quarter is also a centre for artistic expression. Its galleries exhibit a mix of contemporary and traditional artwork, providing insight into the creative pulse of the city.

Deutz

Deutz is well-known for its remarkable mix of old and new buildings. The Hohenzollern Bridge is the most recognisable bridge, studded with padlocks placed by couples as a token of their love. The stunning view of Cologne's skyline, dominated by the stately Cologne Cathedral, is particularly enthralling from this bridge.

The history of the neighbourhood is visible in its cobblestone streets and antique buildings. The 4th-century Deutz Abbey has a rich spiritual legacy, while the Rheinpark provides a tranquil respite for leisurely strolls and picnics. The Rheinische Industriekultur Museum provides insights into the region's industrial progress for individuals interested in industrial history.

Modern Deutz offers a wide range of culinary and recreational opportunities. Diverse tastes are catered to by trendy cafes, historic pubs, and foreign restaurants. The Tanzbrunnen amphitheatre holds concerts and festivals, adding to the lively mood of the neighbourhood.

A short walk across the Deutzer Brücke bridge will return you to the heart of Cologne, making Deutz an accessible and rewarding adventure.

CHAPTER 6: CULTURAL ATTRACTIONS AND OUTDOOR ACTIVITIES

Performing Arts Centres

Cologne has a number of Performing Arts Centres that appeal to a wide range of creative inclinations. These venues, ranging from the modern and inventive to the classic and timeless, provide as a stage for a variety of acts such as theatre, dance, music concerts, and more. The city's commitment to the arts is evident as you see world-class shows, foreign performances, and local talents take centre stage.

The Cologne Philharmonie is one such remarkable venue, known for its outstanding acoustics and holding some of the most beautiful symphonies and classical events. For people who enjoy theatrical experiences, the Schauspiel Köln has a diverse repertory of intriguing plays ranging from modern dramas to reinterpretations of classics.

The architecture of these institutions reflects the variety of performances. Modern constructions coexist with historic structures that have been reinvented to meet current artistic objectives. The combination of old and new contributes to the overall appeal of witnessing art in Cologne.

Art Galleries

The art galleries in Cologne appeal to a wide range of preferences, with an eclectic mix of traditional, modern, and experimental artworks. The city's renowned Museum Ludwig stands out as a refuge for lovers of modern and contemporary art, featuring an extraordinary collection of works by iconic painters such as Picasso, Warhol, and Lichtenstein. Its seamless blend of ancient and contemporary pieces creates an enthralling trip through the evolution of art.

The Galerie Der Spiegel is a must-see for those interested in modern art. This gallery is known for encouraging avant-garde and experimental work, and it pushes limits and challenges preconceptions. Several smaller galleries in Cologne's bustling Ehrenfeld district contribute to the city's status as a destination for young artists and creative shows.

Cologne's art galleries not only exhibit international treasures but also promote local creativity. The creative pulse of the city reverberates within the walls of these galleries, resulting in a beautiful blend of artistic interpretations. Cologne's art galleries provide a window into the city's character, whether you're meandering through the charming alleyways of the old town or immersing yourself in the urban vitality of the Ehrenfeld neighbourhood.

Music Scene

The Cologne Philharmonie, a world-renowned concert hall that offers symphonic performances, chamber music concerts, and contemporary works, is at the core of the city's music culture. Its acoustics and architectural design provide classical music aficionados with a wonderful musical experience.

Beyond classical music, Cologne has a thriving electronic music scene. In the 1970s, the city was essential in the creation of electronic music, giving rise to the influential "Krautrock" genre. Today, venues such as Bootshaus and Gewölbe are internationally known electronic dance music hotspots, consistently showcasing top DJs and generating an exciting atmosphere for late-night revellers.

The local jazz and indie scene thrives at charming venues like Stadtgarten and Sonic Ballroom for a more intimate experience. These venues provide a platform for both local and international artists, establishing a sense of community and artistic interchange.

Cologne's music scene extends beyond concert halls and clubs and into the city's streets and squares. Buskers and street entertainers provide an eclectic blend of tunes to the city, giving a touch of unforeseen magic to the overall musical tapestry.

Festivals And Events

Cologne comes alive in the spring with vibrant festivities. The Cologne Carnival, which takes place in February or March, is a magnificent spectacle in which locals and visitors alike converge to celebrate with parades, costumes and raucous street parties. The RheinEnergie Marathon attracts runners from all over the world as the weather warms, while the International Literature Festival Köln brings together authors and book fans for lively debates.

Summer in Cologne is filled with outdoor events and festivals. The Summerjam Festival, a well-known reggae and global music event, attracts music fans to the Fühlinger See. The Kölner Lichter, or Cologne Lights, is a captivating pyrotechnic display that illuminates the city's skyline against the backdrop of the Rhine River.

Cologne presents the Cologne Fine Art & Antiques Fair in the autumn, a haven for art lovers and enthusiasts. During numerous fall markets, the cobblestone alleys come alive with the aroma of roasted chestnuts, creating a cosy and inviting ambiance.

The city changes into a winter wonderland throughout the winter months with its Christmas markets, the most famous of which being the Cologne Cathedral Christmas Market. Mulled wine, festive decorations, and handcrafted goods create a lovely environment all around town.

Cycling Routes

Along the Rhine River, bikers may pedal beside the scenic waterfront, taking in panoramic views of Cologne's architectural masterpieces including the towering Cologne Cathedral and the Hohenzollern Bridge. As the path goes through attractive neighbourhoods and lush parks, the experience is both relaxing and awe-inspiring.

For the more daring, the city's Green Belt provides a verdant respite from the city's bustle. This route takes riders through lush forests, meadows, and dazzling lakes, immersing them in nature's tranquillity. Cultural riches such as old castles and charming villages dot the terrain, allowing opportunities to pause and soak in the local charm.

Cologne's culture of cycling is well engrained, with well-marked lanes, bike rental options, and bike-friendly infrastructure. The city's level surface allows even inexperienced riders to pleasantly discover its wonders. Cycling is an experience that strengthens one's relationship with the city due to the combination of attractive scenery and physical exertion.

Parks And Green Spaces

The city has a wide variety of parks that cater to a wide range of interests. The Rheinpark, which runs alongside the Rhine River, provides breathtaking views of the city skyline and the gorgeous river. This park is perfect for relaxing hikes, picnics, and even bike rides. The Stadtgarten is a hidden gem for anyone looking for a more historical and attractive experience. It offers a calm atmosphere for relaxation with its beautifully designed gardens, tranquil ponds, and historic structures.

Hiroshima-Nagasaki Park stands out as a striking reflection of the city's dedication to peace and healing. This park not only provides a peaceful haven, but it also encourages reflection on the past and optimism for the future.

Furthermore, green places such as the Volksgarten provide activities for families and groups. These parks bring people together for healthy fun, with everything from playgrounds for children to large open spaces for sports and activities.

Exploring Cologne's parks is more than simply a recreational pastime; it's a means to immerse oneself in local culture and witness the city's dedication to conserving its natural beauty. The city's parks provide a complete experience that compliments the dynamic urban ambiance, whether it's shooting Instagram-worthy images, enjoying a quiet moment of introspection, or partaking in outdoor activities. So, while admiring the city's historical and architectural wonders, don't forget to take time to enjoy the peace and vibrancy that its parks and green spaces bring.

Rhine Boat Tours

These boat cruises allow you to see Cologne's historical attractions from a peaceful vantage point away from the crowded streets. As you float down the river, professional guides provide fascinating commentary, describing the stories behind each landmark you see. The blend of old and contemporary is obvious from the Hohenzollern Bridge, which is ornamented with numerous love locks, to the modern Rheinauhafen neighbourhood.

Daytime and evening excursions are available on the Rhine boat trips. A sunset cruise illuminates the city in a warm, golden glow, providing a romantic environment ideal for couples or anyone seeking a peaceful respite. Daytime tours, on the other hand, are great for families and single travellers, allowing everyone to appreciate the city's history and culture from a new angle.

Rhine boat tours in Cologne appeal to a wide range of interests, whether you're a history buff, a photographer, or simply a traveller looking for a leisurely and educational journey.

CHAPTER 7: COLOGNE CULINARY HIGHLIGHTS

Local Cuisine

The world-famous Kölsch beer, a crisp and refreshing pale ale that is strongly connected with the city's culture, is at the core of Cologne's culinary scene. A Kölsch in one of the city's ancient brewhouses is a must-do, providing a look into the convivial mood of the inhabitants.

Cologne's native specialities extend beyond beverages and include a variety of delectable foods. The hearty Himmel un äd, a dish comprised of mashed potatoes, applesauce and blood sausage, shows the city's ability to mix simple ingredients into flavours that reflect stories of generations past. Another popular dessert is Kölsche Kaviar, a spreadable black pudding that lends a unique flavour to any meal. Cologne's culinary choices do not disappoint anyone with a sweet craving. The Kölsche Quetschekuche, a plum pie with a crumbly topping, and the exquisite Köln-Brezel, a pretzel covered in sugar and nuts, are just two of the desserts that demonstrate the city's dedication to culinary mastery.

Traditional German Restaurants

Cologne's classic German eateries provide a symphony of flavours that echo the city's heritage. The atmosphere at these lovely establishments exudes warmth and sincerity from the moment you walk in. Wooden beams, rustic furnishings, and warm smiles create an attractive ambiance for both locals and visitors. The menus at these restaurants are a veritable treasure trove of culinary classics. Enjoy delectable schnitzels, delicate sausages, and hearty stews—each dish a reflection of culinary skill passed down through generations. Don't pass up the chance to try the famed Kölsch beer, a local brew that pairs nicely with the rich flavours of the cuisine.

However, it is not just about the food; it is also about the experience. Cologne's traditional German restaurants exemplify the spirit of Gemütlichkeit, an untranslatable term that encompasses cosiness, conviviality, and a sense of belonging. You become a part of the tapestry of Cologne's cultural legacy as you sit at a wooden table surrounded by residents engaged in spirited talks.

International Cuisine

The city's food scene reflects its international background, with a diverse range of flavours from cultures from all over the world. As you walk through the cobblestone streets and bustling marketplaces, you'll come across a variety of food alternatives to suit every taste. Cologne's culinary environment is a combination of flavours and fragrances, ranging from traditional German bratwurst stands and substantial schnitzels to tantalising Thai curries and real Italian spaghetti.

With its rustic architecture and cosy cafes, the historic Old Town is a sanctuary for visitors looking for a taste of traditional German foods like sauerbraten and kölsche Kaviar (black pudding). For those who enjoy the exotic, the city's multicultural areas provide an array of international delicacies. Enjoy aromatic Moroccan tagines, the umami of Japanese sushi, or the bright spices of Indian curries.

Cologne's culinary sector reflects the city's openness and diversity, inviting both locals and visitors to sample foreign flavours. Whether you're strolling along the bustling waterfront or exploring the city's secret culinary gems, each meal is an adventure that connects you with cultures from all over the world.

Food Markets

The Wochenmarkt am Kölner Dom, located near the Cologne Cathedral, is a culinary highlight of the city. Stalls loaded with colourful fruit, artisanal cheeses, freshly baked bread, and a selection of meats and sausages can be found here. The market's close proximity to the historic cathedral adds to its allure, providing a magnificent backdrop as you peruse the gastronomic options.

The Rudolfplatz Wochenmarkt is a must-see for anyone seeking a more varied experience. With an array of world delights, this market embraces the city's multiculturalism. The diversity of commodities reflects Cologne's diverse population and international influences, ranging from Mediterranean olives to exotic Asian spices.

Not only is the quality of the items what distinguishes Cologne's food markets, but so is the sense of community they promote. The lively conversations between vendors and customers, the shared love of delicious food, and the welcoming atmosphere make these markets a true representation of Cologne's soul.

Beer And Breweries

Kölsch, a pale, top-fermented beer that is a source of pride for locals, is at the centre of this experience. This crisp and delicious brew is traditionally served in thin, cylindrical glasses, which promotes a sociable atmosphere in crowded beer gardens and cosy taverns. The Kölsch breweries, many of which have been producing this distinctive brew for generations, offer an up-close view at the brewing process and the city's profound attachment to its beer culture.

The sense of camaraderie is one of the most important components of a brewery tour in Cologne. As you interact with residents and other guests, you'll discover that sharing stories and laughs over glasses of Kölsch is more than simply a leisure - it's a treasured tradition.

Aside from Kölsch, craft breweries have established a niche in Cologne's beer market by experimenting with different flavours and styles to suit to changing palates. These establishments provide a contemporary spin to the city's brewing heritage, adding a layer of innovation to the traditional art.

10 Must-Try Dishes

1. **Himmel un Ääd**: This meal, which translates to "Heaven and Earth," combines mashed potatoes ("Heaven")

and apple sauce ("Earth") with blood sausage or liverwurst.

2. This 'Cologne caviar' is actually black pudding garnished with onions and mustard, a wonderful local speciality.

3. **Sauerbraten**: Sauerbraten is a traditional German dish that comprises of marinated and slow-cooked pot roast served with red cabbage and potato dumplings.

4. **Halve Hahn**: Despite its name, which translates to "half a chicken," this dish is essentially a rye roll covered with butter, Gouda cheese, mustard, and onions.

5. **Rievkooche**: Crispy on the outside, soft on the interior potato fritters. Serve with apple sauce or sour cream.

6. **Flönz**: Flönz is a type of blood sausage that is typically served with mashed potatoes and apple sauce.

7. **Reibekuchen**: These potato pancakes, similar to Rievkooche, are frequently

served with apple sauce or smoked salmon.

8. **Weißwurst**: Although not native to Cologne, this Bavarian white sausage is a tasty breakfast option. It goes well with pretzels and sweet mustard.

9. **Döner Kebab**: Because Cologne has a big Turkish community, Döner Kebabs are a popular and savoury street food option.

10. **Kölsch and Himmel un äd Pizza**: Finish your culinary adventure with a local Kölsch beer and a unique spin on a traditional dish, Himmel un äd Pizza, which mixes the flavours of mashed potatoes, apples, blood sausage and cheese.

Wine Tasting

Cologne is home to a plethora of attractive wine bars, cellars, and boutique vineyards that provide a diverse assortment of local and foreign wines. The city caters to all tastes and interests, whether you're a seasoned oenophile or a curious newbie. Many wine tasting establishments offer not just exquisite wines but also educated sommeliers who walk you through each glass, describing the stories of the vineyards and winemakers who put their hearts and souls into every bottle.

You'll be treated to an array of flavours, aromas, and textures that represent the craft of winemaking as you sip your way through reds, whites, and rosés. Beyond the wines, the experience includes the culture and history that have shaped Cologne's relationship with this timeless beverage.

Wine tasting in Cologne provides an intimate interaction with the world of viticulture, whether you choose a cosy cellar tucked within the city's mediaeval walls or a modern wine bar with spectacular river views. It's an opportunity to meet other wine enthusiasts, increase your wine knowledge, and make unforgettable experiences in a city that perfectly blends old-world charm with modern refinement.

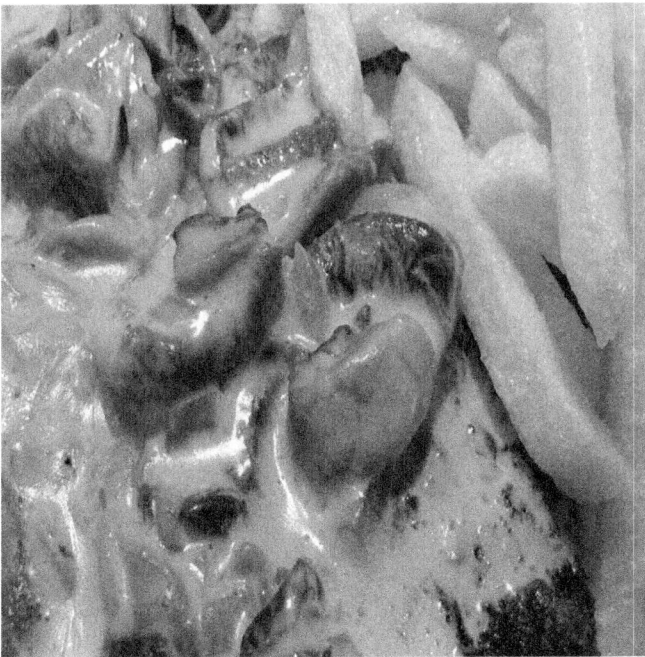

CHAPTER 8: SHOPPING IN COLOGNE

Shopping Streets

- **Schildergasse** is Cologne's most prominent shopping street and one of the busiest in Europe. It houses a diverse range of retailers, from high-street names to designer labels. There are also a few department stores, such as Galeria Kaufhof and Karstadt.

- **Hohe Straße.** is another trendy shopping street in Cologne. It is well-known for its high-end retailers, including Gucci, Prada, and Louis Vuitton. This street also has a variety of mid-range and low-cost stores.

- **Ehrenstraße** is a fashionable shopping strip filled with independent boutiques and designer businesses. It is a favourite hangout for young people and those looking for one-of-a-kind things.

- **Neumarkt** is a pedestrian-friendly square featuring a variety of shops, cafes, and restaurants. It's a terrific spot to people-watch and soak in the ambiance.

- **Mittelstraße** is a high-end shopping strip specialising in clothes and accessories. This boulevard is home to a number of high-end brands, including Chanel, Dior, and Hermès.

Local Markets

- **Wochenmarkt Köln Nippes:** This is a weekly market hosted in the Nippes neighbourhood of Cologne. It is open six days a week and sells fresh vegetables, meats, cheeses, baked products, and other items. Handmade goods and souvenirs are also available.

- **Köln Fish Market:** Every Saturday morning, this market is hosted in the Tanzbrunnen, a concert and event site on the Rhine River. Fresh fish and shellfish, as well as luxuries like oysters and caviar, are available here.

- **Flohmarkt & Antikmarkt Kölner Altstadt**: This flea market is hosted in the Old Town every Sunday. It's an excellent source for vintage clothing, furniture, and other treasures.

- **Weihnachtsmarkt am Dom**: From late November through December, Cologne's famed Christmas market is hosted in the Old Town. With over 150 stalls selling Christmas decorations, food, and drinks, it's a lovely location to meander through.

Boutiques And Designer Stores

- **APROPOS** The Concept Store is a one-stop shopping destination for fashion, beauty, and homeware. Anine Bing, Isabel Marant, and COS are among the international and local brands available.
- **Simon und Renoldi Fashionstore** is a women's boutique specialising in contemporary, independent labels. Ganni, Rodebjer, and Totême are among the brands represented.
- **MATA Cologne** is a women's store that focuses on eco-friendly fashion. Armed Angels, Veja, and Nümph are among the brands represented.

If you're looking for something a little less expensive, Cologne has plenty of fantastic shops. Here are a handful of my personal favourites:

- **Goldig** is a women's boutique that offers a combination of casual and contemporary clothing. Nümph, Fever, and Selected Femme are among the brands available.

- **Magasin Populaire** is a women's clothing store specialising in Scandinavian fashion. Sessùn and Mbym are among the brands represented.

- **Lounge Unique** is a men's and women's apparel business that specialises in vintage and repurposed clothing.

Here are some purchasing recommendations for Cologne:

- The greatest time to shop is during sales, which typically occur in January and July.

- Make sure to haggle! Many retailers are ready to negotiate rates, particularly on things that have been on the shelf for some time.

- If you're looking for something out of the ordinary, go to the Belgian Quarter. A lot of independent boutiques and vintage stores can be found in this stylish neighbourhood.
- When shopping, don't forget to account for VAT (value-added tax). For purchases of more than €175, you can normally obtain a VAT refund.

CHAPTER 9: DAY TRIPS FROM COLOGNE

Düsseldorf

The stately Cologne Cathedral is only a 40-minute train ride away from the lively cityscape of Düsseldorf.

Begin your adventure by visiting the legendary Königsallee, also known as the "Kö." This magnificent street, lined with high-end boutiques and luxury retailers, is a shopper's delight. After some shopping therapy, stroll down the Rhine Promenade, where the river's calm beauty contrasts with the city's lively energy.

The K20 and K21 art museums, which house an exceptional collection of modern and contemporary works, will appeal to art connoisseurs. These galleries, which feature avant-garde works as well as thought-provoking installations, attest to Düsseldorf's cultural relevance.

Explore the Altstadt, or Old Town, for a sense of the city's rich history. Traditional pubs, breweries, and local eateries abound on the picturesque cobblestone streets. Don't pass up the chance to sip Altbier, Düsseldorf's characteristic dark beer, in a centuries-old brewhouse.

The Hofgarten, a gorgeous park ideal for a leisurely picnic or a quiet escape, is a haven for nature enthusiasts. If time allows, a trip to the spectacular Neanderthal Museum just outside of town is a trip through time, exploring human evolution and history.

As the day comes to an end, take in the panoramic view of Düsseldorf from the Rhine Tower. The stunning view embodies the essence of this vibrant city, which is a seamless blend of history, innovation, and cultural strength.

Bonn

Bonn, just a short train trip away, provides an enriching experience that compliments Cologne's metropolitan energy.

Begin your day by leaving Cologne early and getting in Bonn in under an hour. The city, famous for being Beethoven's birthplace, welcomes you with historical beauty. Begin your trip with the Beethoven House, a museum dedicated to the great composer's life and works. Immerse yourself in this renowned figure's musical legacy, surrounded by artefacts and memorabilia.

Explore the alleyways of Altstadt (Old Town), where mediaeval architecture and cobblestone alleys create an exquisite ambience. Don't miss out on seeing the Bonn Minster, a majestic Romanesque cathedral that has stood as a witness to the city's history for centuries.

Stroll along the Rhine promenade and take in the river's tranquil beauty. If time allows, a peaceful respite can be found at Poppelsdorf Palace and its botanical garden. The Kunst- und Ausstellungshalle der Bundesrepublik Deutschland, an art and exhibition hall, presents a varied selection of cultural treasures for a dose of culture.

Finish your day journey with a gourmet exploration of Bonn's food scene. Traditional German restaurants and beautiful cafes provide a sample of regional flavours, allowing you to savour the native food.

As the sun sets, return to Cologne with warm recollections and a stronger understanding for the region's cultural riches.

Aachen

Head out for Aachen, which is only a 1.5-hour train trip away. As you approach Aachen, the historical significance of the city becomes clear:

it was Charlemagne's favourite residence and the centre of the Holy Roman Empire.

The Aachen Cathedral takes centre stage upon arrival. This architectural marvel, a UNESCO World Heritage site, features a unique blend of Carolingian and Gothic styles. The Palatine Chapel within the cathedral bears witness to Charlemagne's influence, with elaborate mosaics and breathtaking artwork.

A stroll through the streets of Aachen reveals its cosy atmosphere and attractive squares. Don't miss the Elisenbrunnen, a neoclassical structure that has been used as a bath since Roman times and offers hot mineral springs to refresh exhausted travellers.

Culinary delights abound, including Aachener Printen, a type of gingerbread biscuit, and substantial German fare. Aachen's market squares also have active markets where you can get unusual items.

As the day comes to a close, you'll be enriched by Aachen's historical treasures, ready to return to Cologne with recollections of a well-spent day.

Drachenburg Castle

Drachenburg Castle is a neo-Gothic architectural wonder perched atop the lush highlands of the Siebengebirge Alps. Its soaring turrets, elaborate façade, and panoramic views of the Rhine River make a really captivating picture. Visitors travelling from Cologne may easily reach the castle by train or boat, going on a scenic tour that highlights the splendour of the German countryside.

Visitors are met by the rich detailing of the castle, which transports them back to the late nineteenth century, when the castle was erected as a private house for a wealthy entrepreneur. Exploring the lavish interiors, which are furnished with beautiful furnishings, rich tapestries, and exquisite stained glass windows, provides an insight into the past's aristocratic lifestyle.

The enormous gardens of the castle are equally intriguing. They provide an idyllic location to wander and appreciate the surrounding natural beauty, as they are meticulously planted with terraced levels, bright flower beds, and quiet fountains.

CHAPTER 10: CUSTOMS AND ETIQUETTE

Language And Communication

- Cologne's official language is German. However, English is commonly spoken throughout the city, particularly in tourist areas.

- If you don't know German, learning a few basic phrases before you go is always a smart idea. This will assist you in getting around and communicating with locals.

- Cologne also has a variety of language schools that teach German and other languages. This can be an excellent opportunity to develop your language skills while also making the most of your trip.

- It is critical to be nice and considerate when communicating with natives. This includes utilising proper language rather than slang or casual words.
- It's also critical to understand cultural differences. Germans, for example, are more reserved than those from other countries. They might not smile or make as much eye contact.

Money And Payment

- Germany's currency is the euro (EUR). At the airport, banks, and currency exchange bureaus, you can exchange your currency into euros.
- Credit cards are frequently accepted in Cologne, but having some cash on hand is still a good idea. Credit cards may not be accepted by all smaller businesses and markets.

- Cologne has ATMs where you can withdraw cash. The majority of ATMs accept Visa, Mastercard, and Maestro. If you withdraw money from an ATM that is not linked with your bank, you may be charged a fee.

- The average monthly cost of living in Cologne is roughly €2,140. Accommodation, food, transportation, and entertainment are all included.

- There are methods to save money in Cologne if you are on a tight budget. You can stay in a hostel, prepare your own meals, and participate in free activities.

Greetings And Gestures

- Greetings: "Guten Tag" (Good day) is the most popular greeting in Germany. This is appropriate for any circumstance, formal or informal.

- "Hallo" (Hello) and "Grüß Gott" (Greetings to God) are two more common greetings.
- Handshakes are a frequent politeness gesture in Germany when meeting someone for the first time.
- When chatting to someone, it is also considered polite to make eye contact.
- It is considered impolite to point with your index finger.Instead, use your entire hand or your thumb to point.
- The thumbs-up gesture is also considered impolite.
- Touching someone's head is considered impolite.

Tipping Guidelines

- Restaurants: A 5-10% gratuity is common. You can either round up the bill to the nearest euro or add a few more euros. Tipping more than 10% is not required, and anything above that is considered generous.

- In bars, a small tip is welcomed but not demanded. You can either round up to the next euro or leave a few euros as a tip.
- Taxis: A 10% gratuity is common. You can round up the fare to the nearest euro or tip a few euros.
- Hotel bellhops and housekeeping employees appreciate a small gratuity. You can donate one or two euros per bag or every day.
- Other services: Tipping for other services, such as haircuts or tour guides, is not usual. You may, however, tip if you believe the service was exceptional.
- Tipping is not customary in fast food or casual eating establishments.

- You can leave a cash tip or leave it on the table.

- When paying the bill at the register, it is not traditional to tip the waiter or waitress.

If you're not sure how much to tip, err on the side of caution and tip a bit more than you think is required.

Social Norms

- Be on time. Because Germans are famed for their punctuality, it is critical to arrive on time for appointments and events.

- Put on appropriate clothing. Although Cologne is a relaxed city, it is still vital to dress correctly for the occasion. In formal settings, avoid wearing extremely exposing or informal attire.

- Personal space should be respected. Germans like to retain their distance from others, so avoid going too near to them when conversing with them.

- Don't be too loud. Germans are often quiet and reserved, so be aware of your volume level when out in public.

- Learn a few phrases in German. Even if you don't speak German fluently, learning a few fundamental words is welcomed. This demonstrates that you are making an attempt to appreciate local culture.

- Tipping is not customary. Tipping is not common in Germany, yet it is greatly appreciated. A little gratuity of roughly 5-10% is adequate.

- Most public places forbid smoking. Most public venues in Cologne, including restaurants, pubs, and cafés, forbid smoking. Outside of these establishments, there are designated smoking locations.

- Be approachable and open-minded. Cologne is a hospitable city, and the residents are generally friendly to visitors. Make an effort to converse with them and learn about their cultures.
- Respect the local traditions. Because Cologne has a rich history and culture, it is vital to observe the local customs. This includes things like appropriately clothing and not being too noisy in public.
- Don't be hesitant to seek assistance. If you need directions or assistance, don't be hesitant to ask a local. Most folks are eager to assist tourists.

CHAPTER 11: ITINERARIES SUGGESTIONS

3 Days In Cologne

Day 1: Visit the Old Town and the Iconic Cathedral

Begin your journey by visiting the UNESCO World Heritage Site Cologne Cathedral (Kölner Dom). Admire its stunning Gothic architecture and, if you're feeling adventurous, ascend to the top for panoramic city views. After that, stroll through the picturesque small lanes, colourful buildings, and bustling marketplaces of the Old Town (Altstadt). Visit the historic Alter Markt square to see the magnificent City Hall and dine at a local restaurant serving traditional German cuisine.

Day 2: Cultural Immersion and the Rhine River

Begin your day in the Ludwig Museum, which is known for its impressive collection of modern art, which includes pieces by Picasso and Warhol. Next, stroll along the River Rhine promenade, which is surrounded with cafes and green spaces. Don't pass up the chance to learn about the history of chocolate making by visiting the Chocolate Museum (Schokoladenmuseum). Consider taking a dinner boat along the Rhine in the evening to see the city from a different angle.

Day 3: Parks, Gardens, and Goodbye

Spend the morning in the Botanical Garden Flora, a tranquil haven with a wide range of plant species and themed gardens. A visit to the Roman-Germanic Museum will provide history buffs with insights into the city's Roman past. Finish your journey with a stroll in Rheinpark, a riverside park. If you have time, ride the

Pänorama cable car for panoramic views of the city and the river.

Family-Friendly Trip

Day 1: Discovering Cologne's Attractions

Begin your journey with a visit to the UNESCO World Heritage-listed Cologne Cathedral (Kölner Dom). Admire its beautiful design and take a lift trip to the observation deck for spectacular city views. Following that, visit the Chocolate Museum (Schokoladenmuseum) to savour delectable treats while learning about the history of chocolate-making.

Rhine River Magic on Day 2

Take your family on a calm Rhine River cruise, which will provide them with stunning views of Cologne's skyline and lovely countryside. Disembark in Rheinauhafen, where you may view the eccentric Kranhäuser structures and take a stroll along the waterfront.

Day 3: Family Fun and Education

This day should be devoted to family-friendly activities. Begin at the Cologne Zoo, which is home to a wide variety of animals from all over the world. Continue to the Odysseum, a science adventure museum that engages both children and adults with interactive exhibits and hands-on activities.

Day 4: Cultural Experience

Immerse your family in the cultural treasures of Cologne. Discover the picturesque Altstadt (Old Town), with its colourful homes, bustling markets, and little stores. Learn about the history of perfumery, a craft steeped in Cologne's past, at the Fragrance Museum Farina-Haus.

Day 5: Relaxation and Parks

Spend the day relaxing in the 9, a lovely urban park. Take a picnic, rent paddleboats, or simply relax in this green haven. In the evening, visit the Puppentheater Köln, a marionette theatre that brings classic tales to life.

Art And Culture Lovers

Begin your journey with taking in the city's architectural showpiece, the Cologne Cathedral (Kölner Dom), a Gothic marvel that has stood for centuries. Its complex intricacies and massive size combine for an enthralling experience.

Then, visit the Ludwig Museum, a haven for fans of modern and contemporary art. The museum provides a thorough overview of artistic developments from the twentieth century onwards, with pieces by luminaries such as Picasso, Warhol, and Lichtenstein.

Stroll through the old Old Town, where picturesque cobblestone lanes lead to the Romano-Germanic Museum, which displays Roman artefacts. The Wallraf-Richartz

Museum, located nearby, offers an excellent collection of European art from the Middle Ages to the nineteenth century.

No art-focused trip would be complete without seeing the Belgian Quarter, a creative hotspot brimming with galleries, boutiques, and street art. Check out the Schauspiel Köln theatre for a taste of avant-garde performances.

Explore Cologne's musical history at the Cologne Opera House, which hosts world-class opera and ballet performances. Alternatively, attend a live concert at the Philharmonie, which is known for its excellent acoustics.

At the MAKK Museum of Applied Arts, you may immerse yourself in contemporary culture through viewing design, crafts, and trends that have shaped modern aesthetics. Kunsthaus Rhenania is an artist-run institution that promotes experimental exhibitions and offers a peek of Cologne's alternative art scene.

Finish your vacation with a calm Rhine River boat, which will allow you to see the metropolis from a different angle and reflect on the creative riches you've uncovered.

Nature And Relaxation

Day 1: Begin your adventure in the famed Cologne Cathedral, a spectacular specimen of Gothic architecture. Take a stroll along the Rhine Promenade, where you can relax by the river, take in stunning views of the city, and watch boats pass by. In the afternoon, visit the Flora & Botanical Garden, a calm paradise with exotic flora and tranquil walks.

Day 2: Visit the RheinEnergieStadion Park, which provides a tranquil setting for a morning jog or a quiet picnic. After that, visit the beautiful Hiroshima-Nagasaki Park, which is dedicated to encouraging peace and tranquillity. Take a relaxing boat ride down the Rhine River to properly appreciate Cologne's natural splendour.

Day 3: Take a day trip to the adjacent Eifel National Park, a stunning natural haven. Hike through lush pathways, breathe in fresh mountain air, and marvel at the pristine scenery. Visit the adjacent Gemünd Vogelsang Area, which is recognised for its rich flora and animals, for a one-of-a-kind experience.

Day 4: Relax completely at Claudius Therme, an amazing thermal bath overlooking the Rhine. Relax and rejuvenate in its hot pools, saunas, and wellness rooms. As the day draws to a close, take in a sunset from the famed Hohenzollern Bridge, which casts a golden glow over the city and the river.

CHAPTER 12: USEFUL RESOURSES

Emergency Phone Numbers

- 112 is the European Union's universal emergency number. It can be used to summon the fire department, an ambulance, or the police.
- The number for the police is 110.
- 116 117: This is the non-emergency medical assistance number.
- The German national health service phone number is 115.
- The German suicide prevention hotline number is 0800 111 01 11.
- It should be noted that these numbers can be dialled from any phone, including landlines, payphones, and cell phones.

Calls to these numbers are completely free.

- When you call, try to be as calm and straightforward as possible.
- Please provide your name, phone number, and the location of the emergency.
- Describe the situation as best you can.
- Stay on the queue until the operator instructs you to do so.

Basic German Phrases

- Goodbye and Hello: Greet residents with a pleasant "Hallo" or "Guten Tag" (good day). When you're ready to leave, say "Auf Wiedersehen" (goodbye).
- Thank you and please: "Bitte" means "please" and "you're welcome." "Danke" is German for "thank you."

- Excuse Me and Sorry: Say "Entschuldigung" (excuse me) to obtain someone's attention. To express regret, say "Es tut mir leid" (I'm sorry).

- Do you speak English? : While many Germans do, it is polite to ask, "Sprechen Sie Englisch?"

- Learn numbers for transactions as well as simple words such as "Wie viel kostet das?" (How much does that set you back?) as well as "Wo ist...?" (Where is...?) to inquire for instructions.

- Food and Drink: Knowing phrases like "Ein Bier, bitte" (One drink, please) and "Die Speisekarte, bitte" (The menu, please) can come in helpful in a city famed for its beer and cuisine.

- Getting Around: Learn transport phrases such as "Wo ist die U-Bahn?" (Where can I find the tube?) as well as "Ich möchte zum Dom gehen" (I want to go to the cathedral).

- Basic Courtesies: The phrases "Bitte" (please), "Danke" (thank you), and "Entschuldigung" (pardon me) are useful in expressing respect and civility.

Safety Tips

- Always be aware of your surroundings. This is especially true in congested areas like public transport or tourist sites.
- Don't flaunt pricey jewellery or electronics. Thieves prefer to prey on those who appear to be prosperous.
- Keep your valuables near you. Even if it's only for a few minutes, never leave your purse or backpack alone.
- Accepting alcohol from strangers should be avoided. Drinks laced with narcotics can put you at risk of being assaulted.

- Avoid walking alone at night, especially if you are in an unknown region. If you must walk alone, keep an eye on your surroundings and stay in well-lit places.

- Believe your intuition. If something does not feel right, leave the situation.

- Carry a personal alarm or whistle with you at all times. This can both deter crime and help you attract attention if you need assistance.

- Keep up to date on local crime trends. This information is available on the Cologne Police Department's website.

For female lone travellers:

- Inform someone of your plans and when you anticipate to return.

- Keep a copy of your passport and other critical documents with you at all times.

- Dress in a way that makes you feel confident and comfortable.

- Be confident and don't be afraid to say no.
- Cologne is typically a secure city, but you should constantly be alert of your surroundings and take care to keep yourself safe.

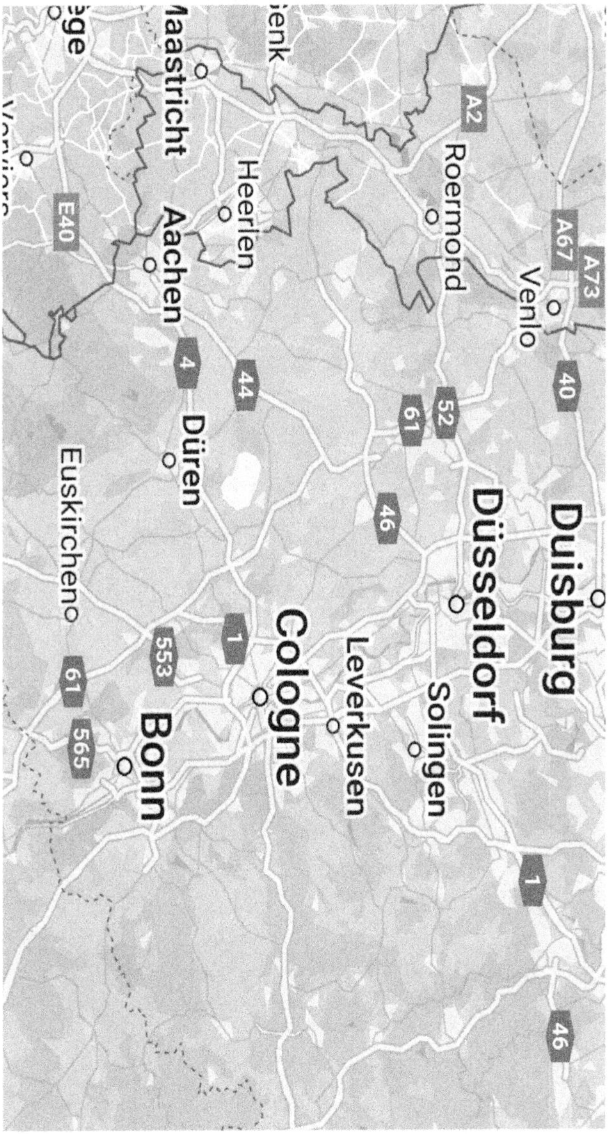
Duisburg
Düsseldorf
Cologne
Bonn
Aachen
Maastricht
Heerlen
Roermond
Venlo
Düren
Euskirchen
Leverkusen
Solingen
A2
A67
A73
E40
40
52
61
44
4
46
1
553
61
565
1
46

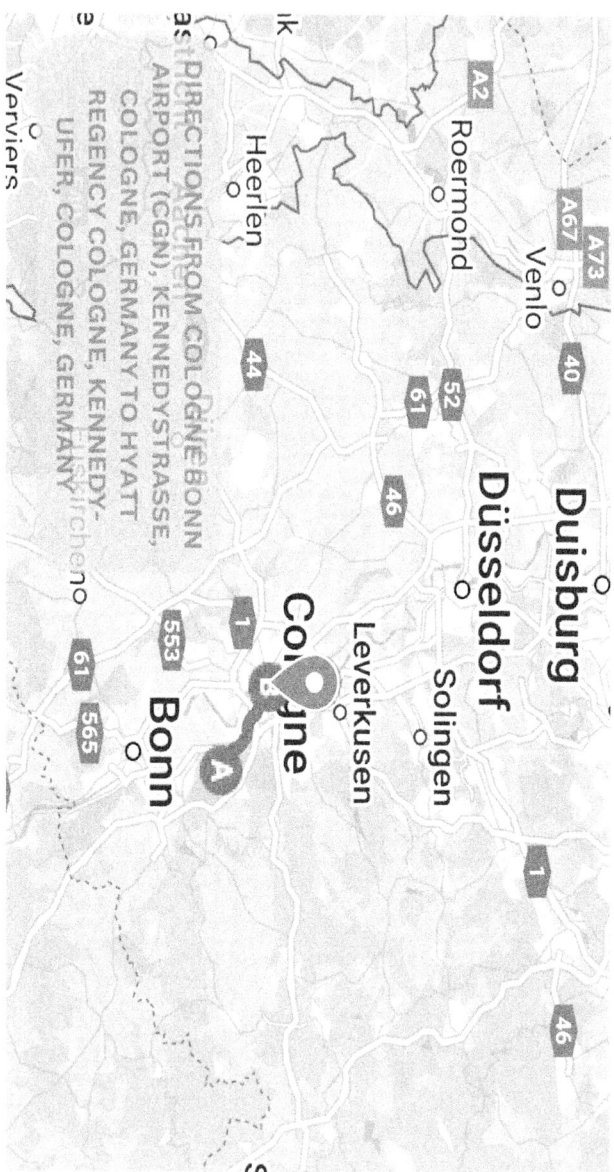

DIRECTIONS FROM COLOGNE-BONN AIRPORT (CGN), KENNEDYSTRASSE, COLOGNE, GERMANY TO HYATT REGENCY COLOGNE, KENNEDY-UFER, COLOGNE, GERMANY

Duisburg

Düsseldorf

Solingen

Leverkusen

Cologne

Bonn

Venlo

Roermond

Heerlen

Verviers

A2
A67
A73
40
52
61
46
44
1
553
61
565
A
1
46

116

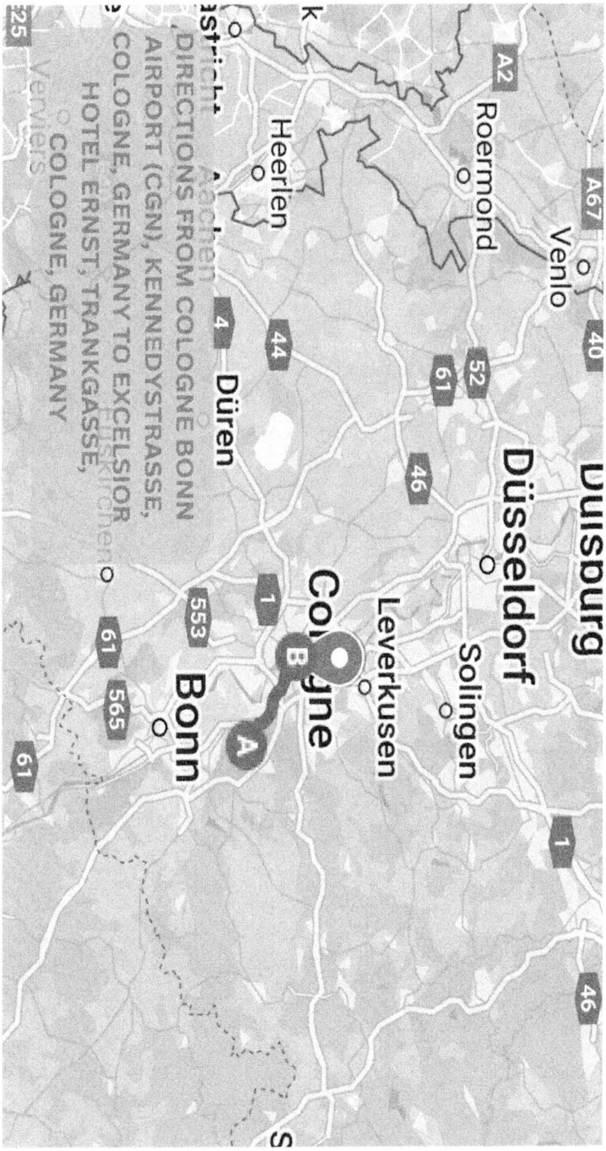

DIRECTIONS FROM COLOGNE BONN
AIRPORT (CGN), KENNEDYSTRASSE,
COLOGNE, GERMANY TO EXCELSIOR
HOTEL ERNST, TRANKGASSE,
COLOGNE, GERMANY

Duisburg

Düsseldorf

Cologne

Bonn

Leverkusen

Solingen

Roermond

Venlo

Heerlen

Düren

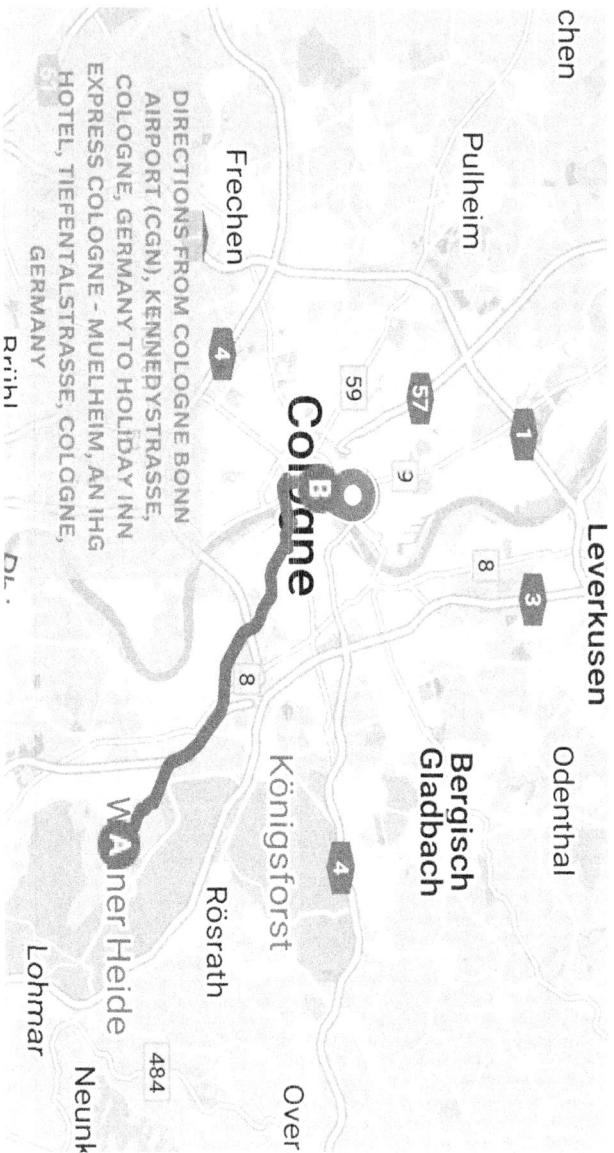

DIRECTIONS FROM COLOGNE BONN AIRPORT (CGN), KENNEDYSTRASSE, COLOGNE, GERMANY TO HOLIDAY INN EXPRESS COLOGNE - MUELHEIM, AN IHG HOTEL, TIEFENTALSTRASSE, COLOGNE, GERMANY

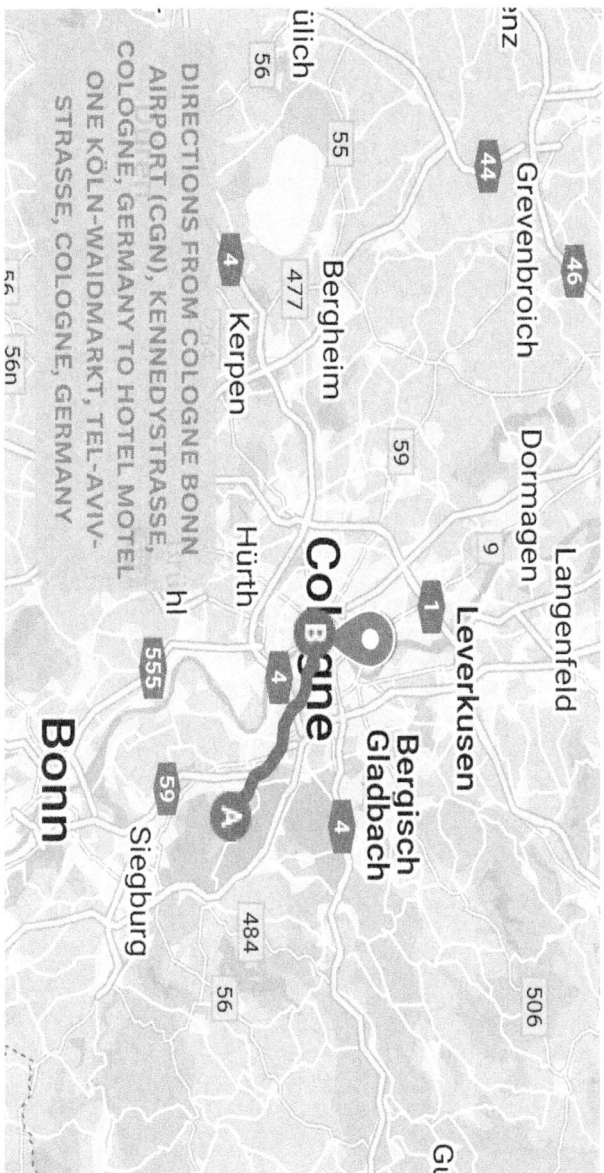

DIRECTIONS FROM COLOGNE BONN
AIRPORT (CGN), KENNEDYSTRASSE,
COLOGNE, GERMANY TO HOTEL MOTEL
ONE KÖLN-WAIDMARKT, TEL-AVIV-
STRASSE, COLOGNE, GERMANY

Printed in Great Britain
by Amazon